becoming sam

becoming sam

Samodh Porawagamage

Winner of the 2022 Burnside Review Press Book Award
Selected by Jaswinder Bolina

Burnside Review Press					Portland, Oregon

becoming sam
© 2024 Samodh Porawagamage
All rights reserved

Cover Image: Mango (Mangifera indica L.):
fruiting branch with numbered sections of flower and seed.
Chromolithograph by P. Depannemaeker, c.1885,
after B. Hoola van Nooten. Wellcome Collection.

Cover Design: Susie Steele
Layout: Zach Grow

Printed in the U.S.A.
First Edition, 2024
ISBN: 979-8-9899577-0-5

Burnside Review Press
Portland, Oregon
www.burnsidereview.org

Burnside Review Press titles are available for purchase from the
publisher and Small Press Distribution (www.spdbooks.org).

Syllabus 13

I. Malli Playing by a Mossy Stone

The Art Lesson	17
Letter from the Back Page at History Class	18
The Next Step	19
The Cost of Flying in the Dark	20
Balancing the Average	21
The Afterlife of Cut Hair	23
Notes on Oblivion	24
A Killing	26
The Wrong Language	27
Regret	29
The Art of Running	31
A Glimpse into Afterlife (after the Bomb)	33

II. Peeling the Mango

Uprooted Elegies	37
becoming sam	39
Growing Kanakambaram in Texas	41
After You, Lakdhas	42
Tonguestruck	44
The Directions	46
Everywhere Love Songs	48
A Definitive History of Quitting	50
Alien Scream	52
My Kinda Name	54
Unseasonal Gardening	55
Illusion	56
Many (No)things about My Being	57
Mirror	60

III. The Monsoons

First Bomb Away	65
The Classic Way of Naming Towns	67
April	69
Airport Memories	71
The Wings	73
Intermission	74
The Postcolonial Dilemma of Taking a Knee	76
Ahnaf,	77
Avurudu at Gotagogama	78
In a Democratic Socialist Republic	79
Anticipation of the Inevitable	82
Lessons Learnt from Hiring Scarecrows	83
Notes	86
Acknowledgments	89

Syllabus

Another day in first grade
when Lalith Sir was typically late
we trapped a gecko—
me, Dinuk, Ashen, the whole lot.

Nobody wanted gecko juice
on his hands, so it came
my turn to cut up its tail.

Because it kept flicking its tongue
through the operation, splayed out
on the teacher's desk, we judged
it was due punishment
for not speaking our language!

I. Malli Playing by a Mossy Stone

The Art Lesson

For grade two weekend homework
Ms. Anoma asked the class to draw
anything we hadn't tried before,
so my friend thought and thought
and drew himself nude in his room.
Everything was in place and quite
normal there, except for a giant
snake where his penis should be.

Authorities acted fast: Ms. Anoma
alerted the principal, and he summoned
the parents to a meeting, deliberated
counselling for the six-year-old
and decided against it. Quite smartly,
they told him: "Just don't draw
anything your eyes can't see."

That solved it: when he drew his neighbor,
Ms. Fatima in her burqa, it was
a draped barrel on top of a box.

Letter from the Back Page at History Class

Dear Saroja,

I pray my paper cranes
one day meet
your paper boats
and never part.

But for that to happen
my paper crane has to crash
or your boat needs to fly.

This morning I realized
why our letters
come opened.
It isn't mum or dad.

My little cousin
thinks his *fleet*
are real planes carrying
cluster, concrete, and other
aerial bombs to shoot down
your camps. For him,
Jaffna is another country
at war with us.

Sometimes I watch
the news and wonder
how he's got it right.

THE NEXT STEP

Force-fed Enid Blyton for months,
I called to Allan Quatermain for help—
the sidekick reporting from Africa
on behalf of my childhood hero,
Sir Henry the extraordinaire:
The one-man army who beheads
glorious wild savages in duels
with punches from his English fist
and marries the rescued
white queens in ceremony to feast
for a year or until bored.

So I, too, wished in secret
to be named after him.
Slaughtering savage warriors
with mum's kitchen knives, I would then
ride on horseback to the farthest
depths of the Dark Continent
with my primitive arsenal and collection
of human skulls. Or dare into a cave
infested with bats on a whim, find
a secret pathway, enter the new world,
and be a citizen. Then leave.

The Cost of Flying in the Dark

Power goes off during Kasun's birthday.
The adults are drinking in the garden.
So they won't let us the kids come out.

We bake in the heat. Someone drops
a candle on the sofa and nearly
sets it on fire. We are fuming

at each other. I consider
punching the coward who keeps tapping
the chair out of fear. Then, a firefly

glides into the room. Everyone hushes
for a second of reverence, as it smooth
sails above the chandeliers

hanging like ghostly fruits. Someone
shouts a challenge. We all know
what it means. A few shadows

climb on the table. I hop on a chair.
We lunge at the flashing light,
our palms flesh coffins.

One falls. He's okay. Then a spoilsport
slaps the light with a magazine and we
get down on the floor for the last rites.

Balancing the Average

If I rank ten or below in grade
six exit exam, my parents agree
to buy me a new mountain bike.

That year, our school enrolls
the best few from a nationwide
merit exam that we old folks
didn't have to take.

They outshine us, and the teachers
like them, but they know well
to stay out of our path. Now and then
we catch one or two stumbling
into our territories and beat them up.

I ace the familiar subjects, but Tamil
language introduced that year adds
only 12 and lets the average down.
Ms. Nanda hands my report card
with the class rank at nineteen.

It isn't only me, so several parents
complain to the teachers. A few
even meet the principal to discuss
the injustice. The teacher
collects our report cards back
and on the last school day of the year
returns them without counting
the Tamil score into the class rank.

When I ask for my bike, mum sighs
like somebody just died and dad
smacks his forehead, yet they agree
to take me shopping this weekend.

The Afterlife of Cut Hair

On the last day of middle school,
I wait for my turn at the barber, watching
his delicate hands cut a girl's hair like he is
preparing salad for dinner—graceful brilliance

striking cut, click, cut, click. I wonder what
the hair feels to be cut-clicked from his hands.
We hack and rack, quell and fell, hew
and unselve the trees, Hopkins wailed

for the poplars in Binsey. Once I thought
the barbers sold cut hair to make
Bombay Muttai. So I kept a close eye
on them like a kingfisher, not pay to eat

my own hair. One day a kingfisher
sat by my pond and I hit him with a tennis ball
on the leg. Off-balance for a second, he then
arrowed past the trees. That week Kingfisher

flew us to Chennai. When I asked what airplanes
had to do with kingfishers, they gave me a special
kids' meal for free. It tasted like uprooted hair
poorly fried in a barber's soothing gel.

Notes on Oblivion

Browning was so tempted to kill
a Porphyria, and once I thought
there would be some beauty in being
a serial killer. She died in his arms, and he knew
she'd be flawless in death. In this love story
on how to separate beauty
from reverence, where does it veer off
into the unacceptable? Once I stole

a strand of hair of the girl
I first kissed. How smoothly it came off
into my palm to the tunes of the sea
in the afternoon!
I'm sure she didn't feel a thing,
though was it Porphyria
she resembled, or Pope's Belinda,
or Sita forced by Rama to suffer
a trial by fire? People moved
backwards that July. A car stopped
and couldn't be revived. A dog with a broken leash
hung around us. We had a tough time

not stepping on baby crabs. A cheeky wave flung
one on to her thigh. We relished how he took an hour
to climb the way down, against my directions.
Back home when I ventured into the grass,
black ants stung my feet. So the oscars
in my pond fought each other to eat
bunches of them and mosquitoes for dinner.
During sleep, I dreamt I had fed them

too many poisonous ants
and snuck out past midnight to check on the fish.
Things turned out fine the next day:
some guilt in the morning
for the gone ants, but the grass calmer, quieter
to walk on. All riots quelled
and peace preserved as if
we can go on living
like the killings never happened.

A Killing

A thief broke into our home and stole
my parents' wedding rings. When the police
brought Lizzy to sniff him down,
I patted her in secret.

Then we all ran after her
crossing the road to a large
garbage bin. She sent it
flying, snatched in her mouth

a stray cat by the neck, shook
it once. Twice. The nine lives
convulsed like the night sky
shot by thunderbolts.

Then she looked at us, flagging
her tail. And stuck the tongue out.

The Wrong Language
after Basil Fernando

A phone rang in the crowded bus to Maradana.
A woman spoke to it in Tamil. People hushed.

The annoying infant stopped crying. Someone yelled
"Bómbayak!" Everybody scrambled to the nearest

door for his life. But Kasun and I didn't want
to lose our seats, so we stayed where we were.

The woman turned to us and said something
in broken Sinhala. We couldn't understand her.

Then, a responsible uncle entered the bus
with a barrage of bomb-proof profanities

and dragged us out of our seats. He ordered us
to stay far away with the rest of the crowd.

Traffic police rushed in. One made a thorough
sweep of the bus. He verified the woman—terrorist

or not—wasn't carrying a bomb at the time.
Yet the policemen praised our due vigilance

against her suspicious behavior. Back in the bus,
other passengers had taken our seats. Together,

they blasted the woman for disrupting
their important travel. So Kasun and I got off

at a traffic light to walk the remaining four miles
to school, feeding our still warm lunch

baskets to a cultish following of stray dogs.

Regret

Perhaps it would have been easier
if you died on your way home

and didn't bump the new car into a column
and leave the door open, didn't knock

into the table and send files flying
as if you were angry with something

invisible. We wanted you to fall,
not collapse, and come to your senses

in a different way. I picture your eyes
seeing everything in red, even my face

with a mask, car stereo hammering
the Big Bang in your head. We saw you

in the shower, wearing the full suit,
and roared outside. Replaying it,

I always drive you to the hospital,
pat your head like

you patted mine
at Avurudu, hold your hand

in assurance. Lifting you to your feet,
we knew all about death

and nothing
about its permanence.

If we knew your goodbye was the puff
of smoke from the ambulance

thinning into the air,
we would have waved.

The Art of Running

Another day that July, a naked thief
had bolted through our garden, the police
and the army in chase: "Horek! Horek!"
they yelled. "Stay away!" So, grandfather
closed the door and pulled the blinds.
According to legend, the lawmen shot
skyward for the scares and tackled him
in the land behind our house.
Then they had hauled him
back to the prison where he belonged.

This is the same month that I was born—
a few years after, not many, ten
at most. Grandfather remembers everything
like this moment, but what he tells
depends on my age, and what he thinks
is okay to share—though that empty lot
still goes unsold, and people never pass
through it after sunset. Tonight, I saw him

plunge into my pond, looking in vain
for a place to hide. During my first
marathon this week, I didn't stop for water
until almost dead on my feet. And thought
it a waste of a precious second to drink
without finishing, before somebody pushed
a bottle into my hands. I couldn't say no.

Here now by the pond, I see his ripples
whisper to the fish. On knees, I dive

my hands into water, reaching for anything
but denial: what could the water mean
after racing against the odds, before
the body falls. Face-down into idealism.

A Glimpse into Afterlife (after the Bomb)

Some fine mist! Now a rainbow,
it's covered me. I'm floating
on my feet, must have
fallen and got back up to take
this path to Nirvana.

Shadows rush like birds
through the clouds, more human
than God. My others. Oh! They wipe
the future off their faces, open mouths
widening at me to turn back.

But I lumber forth. On the walls
there's a host of red flowers. No,
red butterflies. Now they are hatching
everywhere, and in my fingertips

they lose shape and color. Somebody
tugs me from behind. I greet
the angels flapping their wings
as I kneel and collapse in white dust
to the stillness of silence.

II. Peeling the Mango

Uprooted Elegies

I.

On the Colombo beach, I have gazed
over and over again at the sun
ripening before its death,
how the sea swallows it
reluctantly like bitter fruit.
I cannot recall the number
of times I have taken
a crowded bus home after work,
fearing death will come for me

in a public place
where charred flesh
stains walls and pavements for months
after explosions, and families cremate
their loved ones' clothes with a picture

and some flowers placed outside
to wither away in the day's heat
into skeletons.

II.

Here, too, in Texas, when the wind
gets noisier, I hear the familiar ghosts,
who swarmed the footboard
of that doomed bus
hit minutes later by a suitcase bomb,
mutter how lucky I was to
have missed it.

Their faces still come here for me
as winds
pleading elegies for the dead.

But here there are no seas or mountains
or even streams with tiny wild yellow flowers to launch
the souls to rest.

Not even a quiet place to sit
after a full day's work
to watch
the death
of the sun
with an elegy in mind.

BECOMING SAM

My colleagues are cursing the rain
for wet feet and squeaky shoes.
I don't have a grudge against it.
I have come to accept it like
dismembered mice my cat has killed.
I named him "Sam" so that nobody
dares to call me the same.

Yes, naming the cat has been difficult—
name him in English after my captor
to reverse the roles of history?
Go with Sinhala and hope
we'd make a pair, for them
to bite their tongues in spelling?
Would Tamil help, to finally call
my unknown countryman in love?
Or a mixture of all three tongues
just so that he can have
a name for me to call?

Back at home, I had fought with my sister
to name our pets.
Sometimes the stray cats
had ten names in early days
before we settled on two
or three disputed ones. Here my cat
went nameless

for three weeks
before somebody called "Sam"

on a rainy day. I knew it was for me
to share an umbrella and get a name
slapped on my forehead
and pretended not to hear.

Growing Kanakambaram in Texas

A Hawaiian florist in Kahului had a few
Kanakambaram plants to sell, so I almost
flew there to buy one. Over the phone, she felt sorry
for the new migrant, agreed to FedEx a seedling
to Texas at a reasonable shipping cost.

The distressed baby arrived, not even
the size of a finger. In a twelve-inch clay cradle
she grew by the window that winter,
greening the porch in spring and summer, only taking
seven months to fire into flower.

Neighbors loved her. One offered to buy. Many wanted
to know more. A fellow countryman on an Engineering
Postdoc visiting for a conference said: "*Kankabarang*
sounds very Tamil. No way it is the real name
of a plant native to our country. I'll find it for you."

AFTER YOU, LAKDHAS
for Lakdhas Wikkramasinha (1941-1978)

Or is it Lak—*dasa*, you Servant of Lanka?
I recite you mixing the correct portion of home
brews in my tea. I'm not at home, never found

it in a place; literally, I left for Texas,
to rear-append my surname, and naïvely wet
dreaming to teach a wee bit of you to the gen

zeers. There's a temptation here to wipe
my arse in language that I resist. I'm very lost
in poetry, but this is about me, not you. My poem

and how your bruised masculinity curls around it.
You'd have been old, senile, and dying
anyway by now. So there remains

no point coating all my bitter grudges
in brain fluid. No colonialists either,
but worse cobras here. They're called

rattlesnakes. Hot girls behead and skin
them at festivals, such grandeur
of freakish style. People flock in

from all the states, even abroad. Oh how
you couldn't just resist to find one
slithering in the waters of Kelaniya!

Or was it in Galkissa that you died,
bathing shirtless in the sea? I still look
for the now-extinct brand of finest

arrack that empowered you to swim
the forty-six miles to India—as if it matters
that you drowned in freshwater, tap water, or first

in yourself. You see, I was loaned
your books by Cornell, Chicago, Congress,
Harvard, and all of them had

water damage, like you travelled from
Borella Kanatta to piss on them. I'm certainly
not surprised. Malinda writes in his blog

that you were "misresidenced" to God even in
your grave. So wake up, show yourself
or at least the bones. Don't make me dig up

the haunted land. I haven't seen you, so even then
I won't recognize you. There's no photo of you
anywhere. When I Google, Soyinka pops up. Another

reluctant Messiah, sure, but not you. Pan-pan,
let me process the whispered news that it really
is Ondaatje involved in assembling your

selected poems. And if you really must, come
tonight to arson Harvard's copy of *Lustre Poems* lying
on my bedstand. I'll somehow pay for the damages.

Tonguestruck

Yesterday when I Skyped
my mother to whine
how badly I miss my language
here on the U.S. soil
casually she said,
"While you don't have it there,
do miss it!"

Oh, how familiar things
had gone begging:
Once during ninth grade
morning assembly
lightning struck a tree
behind the principal
and we ducked for cover
at the glimpse of the flash
above our heads
before the blast.
And I thought the place
forever smelled sulphureous
yet failed to explain
the colors of lightning
to my American niece.

It was during another walk last week,
someday, sometime, that I walked past
two girls wrapped into their jackets complaining
how Donald Trump has even fucked the weather
off the wall. I understood it too well

and went my way, like I always have, sensing
something odd about it throughout the day.

There wasn't any flash or flare
when amid forlorn reminisces
lightning struck me plumb:
the two girls were talking
in my mother tongue.

The Directions

I ask the kind-looking stranger dribbling
a strawberry ice cream in Central Park
the directions to Colombo, Sri Lanka.
He hasn't been out of the country but faintly
remembers my island's location to be
just below the Maldives
in the shape of a kidney. He then
reconsiders maps of the Reagan era

in his mind against a dog's barking. "I'm sorry
if I've made an error, but my daughter—
she's in high school—wouldn't know
anything about the world. But I guess
you know it'll take you a few
planes to get there." As I weigh his ease
to rethink the mango as a kidney filtering
out nutrients and keeping toxins—and a way
around cutting a mango in two neat halves
to take one half to America—he offers me
a cigarette. I take it and decline
the light. "This won't take me very far."

He agrees. "Are you by any chance
an artist, Sir?" So, I tell him, by routine,
"Don't call me sir, because the British
Monarchy only knighted the local nobility
who fucked up their postcolony. And today
a professor lecturing on East Asian
writing referred to it out of the blue
as Transpacific literature, so I just wanted

to run away and hide from all this
blather that might don a thorny hat
on me. Good guess, though, yeah,
I dabble in poetry. Rootlessness makes me."

"Well," he finishes his cigarette. "Well, well,
well, well." "Well, yeah," I say, "at least
you didn't mistake Dengue for a fellowship
I got from uni, so, well, I think all's well."

I tuck the unlit cigarette behind my ear
and leave. He might do it, too, buying
a map on his way and then blending into
another universe like someone else's protagonist.

Everywhere Love Songs

Part 1: The Kid and the Beetle

On my way to teach love poetry, I see a kid ahead of me with his mum. He couldn't have been three and is already beaten down by the evening fall sun.

He looks back and back at the sidewalk, pointing his finger to the ground. Failing to establish eye contact and smile, I look at my shoes and then at him. Now twisting like a failed firewalker, he keeps showing me the ground between us, forcing his mum to stop.

I follow his directions and see a black beetle. I look back at the kid. He gives me a half-toothless smile and a burst of vigorous nods and then demonstrates how to jump over it.

I give him two thumbs-up and take a longer path to class.

Part II: Later That Night at the Bar

And later that night at the bar, a middle-aged "Jim" sits down next to my loneliness. He tells me his soulmate had given birth to twins. He and she have never been a pair.

I tell him my soulmate and I barely made it through. He has nothing to say to my tipsy theory of one's soulmate having a different soulmate. He asks if I think he's an obsessed voyeur.

I get him a pack of chips and say I write love poetry of all sorts. Distance matters: a proximate sun can burn us. Appreciating a flower without plucking it takes special courage. I also tell him about the kid and struggle to construct his as an act of love.

He laughs and tells me that I don't sound or act like an Indian. Then he nods and leaves. Later, the barmaid tells me Jim had already paid for everything I bought that night.

A Definitive History of Quitting

Just a teen, semi-supervised,
once I detonated a bomb
to see how parts explode with fire
into other parts.

Most nights at home after camp,
I woke in fear of shooting
my dog in the head, but then he'd jump
on the bed and lick my face.

Others thought I had loved
Defense College until one day in training
I tightened my grip too much
around NK34's neck and he

nearly swallowed his tongue.
The silence of taking him
to the hospital in a lorry
felt like it's nothing

to quit—just duty and having
excelled at it. Later, the uniforms cleared me
and diagnosed some condition in him.
He even called to apologize and, from his stammer,

I knew who was behind it.
On leave, I wrote a whole book within days
and never took to memoir.
My father, the Colonel, visited to tell

a stray cat he used to feed
had gone missing. Dad stayed optimistic
like only he could.
I imagined the cat stepping on a landmine

and bursting like a balloon.
It was found dead in a well and I wondered
what dad did with it.
Mum said pre-school me insisted

burying dead fish in water
not knowing what it meant,
as if buried in-ground the fish, surely,
wouldn't be able to swim.

Alien Scream

Has technology made us
fear magnification?
Everyone wants to be seen through
the other's limited vision, not when
it's amplified. Perhaps that's why
when I'm filming on my phone nobody minds
being recorded, only passersby waving
at the camera. But how dangerous

the binoculars are: the first time I tried to spot
a tiny bird on campus, a policeman had waited patiently
behind me until I finished. He said there was nothing
wrong with what I was doing, but that he, too, would
freak like a freshman if I focused on him—
his words, not mine, though I can't remember
the exact words of the apartment security guard
the night he was woken by calls
from concerned citizens that I was sniping
on them that starry night. They swore to him by God
a crosshairs had run through their bodies.

A police cruiser came screeching to a halt.
The officers quickly reassessed my gear.
Yet they requested a sweep of my place
for the weapons of mass destruction.

Then everybody convened and preferred
that I stargaze somewhere else for a while.
So I went inside to Netflix the entire
Alien franchise that night, but fell asleep

halfway and agreed to model for Edvard Munch
revising *The Scream.*

My Kinda Name

It's February. Too lazy to cook, I've ordered
Free Delivery! App pings and he knocks.

The poor guy's in a parka. Two feet away,
I can't see his face. The food's steaming.

He's just made my day. "Sorry, I'm a few minutes
behind," he says. "The roads are crazy with snow.

I saw four accidents today." Then he tries
my name on the bag: "Jeez! Zamudd, Sha-

mouth, Chamoth, no, Saa-mutt, right?
Haha! See, I can. But dude, seriously!

where in hell… what kinda name is that?"
"Oh, it's a Vedic mantra the ancients chanted

for rain but also means I'm the king,
can lead well, or be vicious. It's actually

a Fuck-off kinda name. Thanks anyway
for asking." Then I take the food.

Step inside and lock the door. Skip
rating the service. Tip ten dollars.

Unseasonal Gardening

My lover visits for Thanksgiving. Her heart
isn't for Texas, but I'm working and can't move
for a while. "Maybe a plant or two can lighten up
the house," she says taking leave. I drop her
at the airport and drive to the florist. Of course,
they don't sell live plants. I hear the shop girl
chuckle to her friend. I walk away

to the *nursery* off the corner, quite concerned
they would sell me a child. As usual, somebody
hastens to prevent theft. I ask him for an indoor,
low-maintenance flowering plant, one that I can't
kill in a week. "A perennial or an annual?"
he says and I wonder what color they are, or
was that a question? "Please show me." He points
to an area in blooms. "Which season would you like
your plant to flower?" I remember

my mother's garden, beaming every day in orchids,
roses, and many flowers I didn't bother
to learn to name. I pick one like Araliya, shake
my head: "We don't believe in seasons."

ILLUSION

Tonight, we watch
The Great Conjunction—
Saturn waltzing into
the heat of Jupiter,
a cosmic replica of kissing
on Skype: you know, the planets
are a million miles apart,
we are on different continents,
and we bank on the eyes
to make it real.

Many (No)things about My Being

1. The Westernization of My Brain

There're no hideouts from knowledge
when it comes, nonstop, persistent
onto you, to reconsider what to do next.
Get painlessly brainfucked, as if
there's no other thrilling prospect
to find outside reason; oblige
and bury your legacies six feet
under that rational crust
with questions and doubts!

11. The Sentimentalization of My Heart

This V Day emphasis is on gifts—
roses, chocolates, perfumes, dresses
as ones that will tickle,
fill and hold her heart
with love only for me—
if regularly done
with sweet words, like neo-Prince Charming
for colonial Disney Princess.
Let's grow old, Luv,
in perfumed, rose-filled, chocolate beds
(assuming nonstick) and care
nothing for the stinky
world outside.

Lurve will overcum the rest!

III. The Viagrization of My Dick

My dick is insignia
of my masculinity!
Not at the natural peak
but when it's fueled
with performance enhancers
and newer tips for better fucking
(thanX online purchases).
Ayurveda helps, too,
and watching newly released
3D Porn
with eXXXtra scenes
drives us, back-to-back,
to Heaven.

MIRROR

Looks like I can't win you over
                         with poetry—that's good!
It should stay that way. I wish
                         we could clink our empty hearts
like our glasses, so the melting ice
                         can sweeten the leftovers.
          You are
sighing to me about the horizon;
                         it has gone dark to our inattention.

    But lights of the returning
                         fishing boats have lit up my world—
    so tiny, they could be the still
                         pulsing hearts of fireflies,
    resisting siren calls to give up
                         and crash into the marine universe.
          Your hair
    is rising on to the breeze, crowned
                         with the glow of the fleet. This is why
    everybody needs a mirror held
                         up to them, and to hear MØ
    pleading *don't let this be our*
                         final song in the background.

III. The Monsoons

First Bomb Away

A bomb escaped
leaves not a bang, but a frozen
silence in the ears.

Once we lived
so close to too many
to know the difference.

One of the worst took
a school baseball team
on their way to play
for an easy away win.

Then they were so regular
that everybody lost count

and were suspicious of all
women "with child."

That's how they prey on
your sympathy, the President
thumped his chest. We voted.

Mum and dad worked the same hours
half a mile from each other.

Every day they left and returned
on different routes to save me
a parent, just in case.

At thirteen, I had my luck to miss
a doomed bus

when a snotty street kid
selling something like
incense-sticks

blocked my run
to the trafficked bus.

A rival schoolboy
mocked me from the footboard

and I cursed him to fall and break a limb!

Next, a different silence
kept ticking for a decade

for six more
within hours
on Easter

on my lover's birthday.

Happy Birthday, I said
in American comfort.

She pretended not to hear
and cried on my shoulder.

I hid the gift
and never took it out again.

THE CLASSIC WAY OF NAMING TOWNS

Carbon testing reveals that one of Cornell's overlooked acquisitions, an ancient Pali manuscript on a palmyra leaf, is older than 1,200 years. After I struggle a whole day to decode it, my new friend, Harry, takes me to a dingy bar with upbeat music to tell me all about Ithaca. I spend four dollars on a Long Island Iced Tea and a more worthy half of it to play "Karma Chameleon" on the jukebox. Harry says Ithaca's more colorful and quainter than "Karma Chameleon."

He says that George Washington assigned lands after a war to some classically educated generals, and they named the provinces to reflect that education. *Every day is like sur...vival.* So, the Algonquin word Taughannock became Ithaca. I repress my urge to play Sia's "Chandelier."

I See a Bad Moon Rising! Harry is adamant the manuscript was hastily written with conquest imminent: "Always...something wicked that way comes from Indi...yarrr?"

"It says to seek shelter in temples—not frickin' caves like during wartimes."

"Maybe they tried to erase it?" I search the ceiling in vain for some moonlight.

...I hear the voice of rage and ruin, says the last drop of my Long Island. Inside me, it wants to talk anything but the classics.

I say how my town came into being. The land was unfit for export cultivation or to be a Cricket field. During the Second World War, there was an influenza epidemic. And the Japs bombed Colombo for fun. They took out the whole Angoda hospital in minutes. *Looks like we're in for nasty weather / One eye is taken for an eye.*

Not our war, I say. Harry asks my Facebook handle. But the influenza epidemic worsened, and the Poms had to open a new hospital in the middle of nowhere. They named it the Infectious Diseases Hospital.

"Do you want to go dancing somewhere with college chicks?" *Oh, don't go 'round tonight / It's bound to take your life.* More died from starvation than from the influenza. So, a few people started shops around the Infectious Diseases Hospital—which thrived. More people came. They called the place IDH for short, but pronounced it *Aydiyech*.

Adele screams *Hello!* without realizing by then we have spent more than 10 hours together.

"Ithaca and IDH," I sigh. Adele tries to match it in a wail.

"Let's go to Moonies," Harry says, getting up.

APRIL

        The whole country is a battered body, marked
     with limbs denied thirty days of blood.

Only

     it's there; an earthy vitality still feeds the broken
        branches swaying to the monsoon.

                         Strange beasts

        have roughened up this body. Some are invisible,
     most without pawprints, and they have feasted on

our forests

     for so long that they have destroyed
        the ecosystem: The trees aren't green.

  Their leaves

        have long left us. No new buds break this April.
     What is blossoming to them? Where is

our birdsong

     in the misty skies? My love, we aren't holding
        an umbrella in the downpour—it might block

     our flawless

        view of the sky. How is it wrong to blink
     through this daily dejection and shout for

the brilliant

     flash of real dreams lining up at the horizon, taking over
        as the clouds disappear? Those

                       flimsy mountains!

        In the rain, I'm not holding you, you aren't holding on to me. We are dry leaves feeding our own roots.

So when

        you tell me in tears that we shouldn't love
            each other right now for the sake of future

            I know it, too.

AIRPORT MEMORIES

At an airport, as you wait your turn,
the skin makes you judge
yourself before others enact
your judgement. Expecting the worst is as real
as you always imagine it. Once in Düsseldorf,

I was sitting on my own, and somebody just
walked up to ask for my passport. I looked at
his eyes, asked, "Who are you?" and he
melted away before I processed
something real was happening. Vigilante

or mugger, credentialed or not, there is proper
planning to this. It's also methodical
when the buzzer rings to choose you
for an additional screening—always the case
if I shave my head because I look

very military. Airport Security at Dallas
asked if I am military and I said, yes,
I once have been. He nodded
in vague solidarity. People assume
a lot and things go too far. When I'm sitting

by myself, it becomes about life
before death. I practice the art of raising
my hands to the guns, so that nobody
panics enough to shoot—something
they don't teach you anywhere. Open-eyed

during overnight transits, I wonder if the colors
redeem themselves. Then, outside, I forget
to wonder more. But last night my woman
asked if I'd still like the dove
tattooed on my forearm. I didn't want

more dark on me than my inheritance,
so my skin folded shamefully like a sinner.

THE WINGS

Nobody comes here to be alone.
Some birds kept watch, but they
too have flown away for the winter.

I lie on the grass, aim my Celestrons
at the sky. Nothing moves. The world
is no longer alive. Campus police

drives by. She waves. She's used to
seeing me here. I move under a tree,
prick my nose to a smell so familiar:

torture and blood. Under a thick bush,
a pair of wings strewn from each other.
The grass has perked up with dry blood.

The claws are curved into a ball as if
they grabbed the air against the pain.
The feathers are intact, not a speck of blood.

I want to bring the remains home, give
a proper burial, or let them display his pride
well after death. Campus police kneels beside me.

The wind picks up. The wings sway to fly,
but the claws keep them grounded.
We reflect on the precision of violence.

INTERMISSION

I assume you are stranded without a way
to escape Galle Face Green, or rather

trying to get there. You tell me that subscriptions
to text alerts issued by embassies

direct you to your next article. I agree it takes
getting lost to getting it right in differently

colored faces, alleyways, black hair.
Then, I stop to reflect on my people,

whose eyes are so sealed in skin that we'll
soon need archeologists to retrieve

the deposits of anguish buried in them.
You don't look me straight in the face.

Instead, you blow on your tea. "I'm from England,"
you say, looking out the window. A sunbird

flutters outside. It could be your soul. Your orb
bleached out of white skin. I feel like Changez.

In the silence, we avoid discussing the obvious
subject of it. I offer to take you there.

You accept, with a bright smile, and I feel sorry
for both of us. "Finish your tea," I say.

"It's a delicious cup of Ceeylon tea." Your trochaic
Ceylon reminds me why the island is drowning

in a sea of loans, though this is not the hour
for metrical animosities. The udavadiyas

still hold their peacock blooms
at the next-door florist, as the sunbird

keeps clawing at his reflection in the window.

The Postcolonial Dilemma of Taking a Knee

Jason asks if I'd like to take a knee
before we begin a game of chess. We are outside
by a duck pond in spring. I have quarantined
for two months. A white girl walking her Doberman
winks at me. A George Floyd protest on 20th Street
shouted as I drove past, and I honked in solidarity. It is

different here. People are walking, jogging, some
youths playing basketball. I wonder if they did it, too,
and my friend, having come early and seen it, feels
the pressure to repeat it. I want to kneel
for the Black lives, the whole minority, myself
in Texas; include the Tamil and the Muslim back home.
There is no difference here or there: when it is not

your time, it is your life. My conscience resists
kneeling before the oppressors again, resists interpreting
taking a knee that way. The ducks are gawking. Our armies
await command in black and white. "Let's do it on both knees
before we start killing," and Jason stares into my face.

Ahnaf,

It's just been a year? Let's wait a couple more.
Then, you'll be out for a bit. Don't expect
more than that: you can walk up to the shop
by the prison. Light up a cigarette and be
arrested again on the charge of conspiring

to blow up the high court two bus stops away
with cigarette smoke. In case you don't
smoke, don't run home. Running while
non-Sinhala is no longer permitted and came
into effect during your detainment. Shit, I say

that now as a compliment! One day I will
smack my head for this. Try to burn my hair
in water. Both dangerous options. To be honest,
I didn't know about you. Nor did I come back
to rescue you. On imagined debt, I came to serve up

whatever for the flourish of verse. Now it's
pointless to stick to the plan. Soul searching
is for the soulless to fill a void. And shame's
the word my generation will not recover from
for writing every other verse on Instagram.

Avurudu at Gotagogama

I watch you, my love, swimming
in the dreams. Ghostly vessels,
disguised as their own subtle
reflections, tear at your skin.

Before the sun's epiphany—the night—
borrows the island, I too would like to stick
my hand in the flesh. Pull out
the ripe fruit, preserve us
a shadow paradise. Then worry needlessly
about presentation. It seems
the normal thing to do in makeshift
times as these, where hate

spreads beyond the mapped depths
of history—third gen born to colonial
sins. This morning when the past
bled into our throats in schools

of strange fish, I wanted to
kiss you, the morning, the words,
reluctantly spinning earth.
Swat away the flies. Celebrate.

In a Democratic Socialist Republic

Seventy-two years of Democracy spent
crossing the bridges, climbing the hills,
crushing wars and rebellions.

We waged
a *humane operation*
against terrorism
and the world
didn't mind.

Now, let us peacefully enter
a new chapter
of the same old book.

"You traitor, international plotter,
now we can safe-travel in buses
and trains, the LTTE is demolished!

Here malli, don't publish this in your newspaper:
bombs don't terrify me now
but they haunt my every travel,
I mean, the ticket officers, malli.

Ah yes, my wife doesn't manage
household things so easily now
but who cares, my sons have a country to live."

Our public servants have started
once again to beam at us
on roadside walls and posts

scorching in the sun, dripping wet in the rain
cutthroating for the Best Smile Award.

And the Police, our benevolent
khakied gentlemen,
ever so kind,
massage our rebellious heads
with cushioned batons.

The rebel
sent to the rehabilitation camp
(called the C.I.D.)
hangs himself on a beam,
unable to betray his conscience.

I see in a ditch
the goddess of law—
that good-for-nothing whore
pleading for her life
again to survive
to drag down the development.

(Protest:
"Decapitate the bitch
with a single whack of the sword
called justice
don't let her confine
our sane politicians
to her comfy bed.")

We climb
a rusty ladder
one rung at a time

to another Democratic
Socialist planet
only visible
in the dark
at night.

Anticipation of the Inevitable
    at the IUSF Protest, 20th May 2022, Colombo

Bloody doesn't capture their blood. Bloody,
here, was an end, though their blood hasn't stopped
bleeding despite they are bloody. It's maybe
bleedy, then. Or blooding. Or bolding. Nothing
stops their valves from carrying on bleeding
until they drain, or are drained by force, before
being drained anyway. So tonight, I was there

to bond—not close, not almost—with them
in flesh to see living proof of the police
putting our tax money to best use: to reassure
the government of the country's essential medicine
for protesting. High-pressure water cannons
couldn't move them. Someone joked
the President could deploy water cannons to solve

the droughts in Rajarata. They cackled in wait
to be teargassed as the veterans of suffering, barely
two decades into life, our boys and our girls. Our
clergy, too. I laughed at their jokes and watched
our bleeding flow: Out. Out. Hot. Hot again

Lessons Learnt from Hiring Scarecrows

We hired 'em protect our luscious paddies. 'em
dam'n scarecrows. Not all at once. Jus one,

first time. From those big cats. Who we
thinked gonna eat our harvest and set

fields on fire. Our luscious paddies. Our green
luscious paddies. Was many-a-many

green seas of them, nodding 'em golden little heads
like lasses in Apriyel. First scarecrow,

we built'im from scratch. Used up all stored supplies
of hay. Such dapper uncle then, we give him

mustache and tie, that he wrap around
his neck. & fine job he did, 'em spotty cats

now growl'd faint from forests far. Lemme get
my brothers help, he say, 'em rusting

doing nothing. Sacred in duty like me, he say. *We*
banish 'em cats once and for all & for-ever

he say. We greedy lot! You form an army and chase,
say'd we. Partied with'em most of we.

Come see, come see, they call one glory morn.
Big cats banished we. Not one them silly

pawprints we find in mud. But our Hon. Scarecrow—
what fine scarecrow he was—says he sees 'em birds

stealing into fields now. From other country
he say, snatch your vee karal whole, O, no

your best golden lasses they take, he say. Increase me
power, he say, O! let mee take the bastards down.

All it good! We hire 'em back, the wholesome bunch!
Wonky lads say em s'crows hide some harvest

in far other fields. But we men like our rare piece
of mind. & same old, same mold
we know to trust. Only they don't give
us enough now... Tell us it take time.

But we look, all round the nooks. They've
trampled our rice plants. Keep giving

us less and lesser. And act like his clan
—'em walawwa scarecrows—

own our paddies. So, we sen' em packing
home. Only they resist, now that

too many 'em buggers. We din't pay so they
had to leave, those cunning scarecrows.

Or they pretend. They don't go, but camp
on the road by our paddies, blocking others

to be hired again, Hon. Scarecrow, fourteen
years into pension. His brothers, same
old, same mold, but them we ain't quite seen;
all wait snarling at us now like em big cats

they banish 'emself. New paddyhead, though,
give us better reaps. Now it look all

our old luscious green. Then one daylight
he let some crazy beasts, him. Let'em

ruin one paddy whole. Make us never safe
again. Never safe in our own paddies. So

we call in the same old same mold. Like us
same old, same mold as 'em

to suffer our same old, same old, and nothing
more. Next thing we learn is we got no more

paddies. Nor do our caretaker scarecrows. They
had sold them abroad. That's why we fighting

'em scarecrows war. Families of 'em, blocking us
off our barren paddies,

our once luscious green paddies.

NOTES

"Malli Playing by a Mossy Stone": "Malli" is little brother. The phrase "by a mossy stone" alludes to William Wordsworth's poem "She Dwelt among the Untrodden Ways."

"The Next Step": Enid Blyton was an English children's author. Allan Quatermain is the narrator—rather than the protagonist—of a popular series of Lost World novels written by the English writer H. Rider Haggard. Ngũgĩ wa Thiong'o calls Haggard a "genius of racism."

"The Afterlife of Cut Hair": See the poem "Binsey Poplars" by Gerard Manley Hopkins. "Bombay Muttai" is a Sri Lankan variety of cotton candy. "Kingfisher" here is a low-cost (South Asian) regional carrier.

"Notes on Oblivion": This poem refers to "Porphyria's Lover" by Robert Browning, "The Rape of the Lock" by Alexander Pope, and the Sanskrit epic poem *Rāmāyana* by Valmiki.

"The Wrong Language": "Bombaya(k)" is the Sinhala word for a bomb. It is a Sri Lankan superstition that a string of unending profanities can ward off/delay the evil.

"Regret": Avurudu is the traditional Sinhala and Tamil new year in Sri Lanka that falls in mid-April.

"Peeling the Mango": Mango here refers to the shape of Sri Lanka on the world map.

"Uprooted Elegies (I.): The description in the opening stanza draws inspiration from *Salalihini Sandesa*'s stanza 48.

"Growing Kanakambaram in Texas": "Kanakambaram" is a Malay term, not Tamil. It is mispronounced by the other character as "kankabarang." The plant is also called firecracker.

"After You, Lakdhas": Lakdhas (also Lakdasa) Wikkramasinha (1941-1978) is one of the most influential Sri Lankan and postcolonial poets. In Sinhala, "Lakdhas" means "Servant of Lanka." The poem contains subtle references to a few of his poems. Borella Kanatta (aka the Borella Cemetery) is his resting place.

"The Directions:" In the world map, Sri Lanka is ABOVE—not below—the Maldives. "thorny hat" is a reference to an advanced degree.

"Everywhere Love Songs (PART II: Later That Night at the Bar)": But then, I'm not Indian.

"Unseasonal Gardening": "Araliya" is the Sinhala word for a Sri Lankan variety of frangipani/plumeria plant.

"First Bomb Away": A reference to the populist Mahinda Rajapaksa who, in 2004-05, would go on to build a genocidal, divisive, and highly corrupt political regime till 2015. The Easter Sunday Bombings in 2019 targeted several churches and hotels. 269 died.

"April": In April 2022, protests—eventually successful—emerged to bring down the Rajapaksa government.

"Intermission": Galle Face Green was the epicenter of said protest movement. Changez is the narrator and protagonist of the anti-imperial—rather, the reverse imperial—novel *The Reluctant Fundamentalist* by Mohsin Hamid. Ceylon was the name for colonial Sri Lanka and is pronounced with an iamb. Udavadiyas are a Sri Lankan variety of orchids.

"Ahnaf,": Ahnaf Jazeem, a Sri Lankan Muslim poet writing in Tamil, was detained for over a year in prison under the emergency law on charges that his poetry incites racial violence. To learn more, and to read translations of Jazeem's work in English, visit freeahnaf.wordpress.com.

"Avurudu at Gotagogama": "Gota" is the nickname for the president of Sri Lanka. Gota-Go-Home was a makeshift village erected in Galle Face Green by the protestors to bring down the Rajapaksa government.

"In a Democratic Socialist Republic": The poem refers to the end stages of the Sri Lankan Civil War in which many atrocities and human rights violations were committed. C.I.D. is the Criminal Investigations Department of Sri Lanka Police, notorious for its violent methods such as torture and regular extrajudicial killings on false pretenses (+ resulting prisoner deaths and suicides).

"Lessons Learnt from Hiring Scarecrows": "Scarecrows" here collectively refers to the family dynasty of the Rajapaksas, headed by Mahinda Rajapaksa himself. "cats" refers to the Liberation Tigers of Tamil Eelam (LTTE). "vee karal" is Sinhala for mature rice seed heads. "'em walawwa scarecrows" is a reference to the Rajapaksa family's feudal nobility.

ACKNOWLEDGMENTS

Annasi & Kadalagotu: "Many (No)things about My Being"

Another Chicago Magazine: "After You, Lakdhas"

Mantis: "The Classic Way of Naming Towns"

Pine Row: "The Afterlife of Cut Hair"

Poetry Northwest: "Letter from the Back Page at History Class"

The Saltbush Review: "A Definitive History of Quitting"

"My Kinda Name" and "The Wings" appeared in the anthology *Out of Sri Lanka: Tamil, Sinhala & English Poetry from Sri Lanka & Its Diasporas* (Bloodaxe Books).

Samodh Porawagamage's first book, *becoming sam*, was selected by Jaswinder Bolina as the winner of the 2022 Burnside Review Press Book Award. He writes about the 2004 tsunami, Sri Lankan Civil War, poverty and underdevelopment, and colonial and imperial atrocities. His poems have appeared in the anthology *Out of Sri Lanka: Tamil, Sinhala & English Poetry from Sri Lanka & Its Diasporas* (Bloodaxe Books) and a number of journals.

"A vivid, gutting, and memorable collection, *becoming sam* moves from poem to poem like a deftly crafted memoir in verse. It recounts, both, the quotidian dramas and violent terrors of a childhood lived through the Sri Lankan civil war alongside the quieter violences committed against an immigrant acclimating to life in the U.S. The subtle shocks and startling turns in Samodh Porawagamage's poems bring me sometimes to wonder, sometimes to tears, and always to gratitude for their brilliance."

—Jaswinder Bolina

"How does one survive diaspora? Or rather, what does one become, carrying the home country while you live in someone else's land? In *becoming sam*, Samodh Porawagamage offers us a poignant memoir in verse that takes us from his earliest memories in Sri Lanka to his current life in Texas, where he lives but is never entirely at home. Sri Lanka is around every corner of his mind, as he hears the news from abroad of protests and change: 'We are dry leaves feeding our own roots.' His poems testify both to the ignominies of immigrant life—from mispronunciations of his name to airport security patdowns—and the secret wisdom of being an outsider with equal parts wit and pathos."

—Philip Metres

"Samodh Porawagamage's poems are fast-moving, thrumming with both spoken energy and formal finesse. His lyrical bulletins from Sri Lanka tell us things that our parochial news and literary cultures have no time for. A truly cosmopolitan, transnational sensibility has arrived, conversing with Sri Lankan poets (notably Lakdhas Wikkramasinha) and speaking back to, and alongside, the Western canon."

—Vidyan Ravinthiran